Patrick J. O'Connor

Words into Worlds

Published in Ireland by
Oireacht na Mumhan Books
Coolanoran
Newcastle West
Co. Limerick

The aid of research funding
from the University of Limerick
is gratefully acknowledged

Printed by Litho Press Co.
Midleton, Co. Cork.

Word  *Worlds*

For Nuala

In the beginning was the word

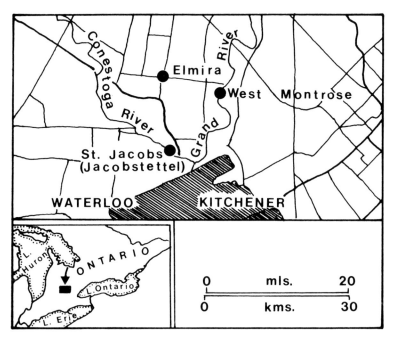

Mennonite country, south western Ontario

Horse and buggy: the old order stayeth

Mennonite Country

A satanic figure
in driving rain
cuts straight
through the noon day,
woman, horse and buggy
- a triad in strained motion -
is powered by fury along
the road to Jacobstettel.

Through into the village
there is no abatement,
in the wrath of heaven,
in the clouded overload
that pours upon
meeting-place, forge and store:
integrators in a world
moving to its own sombre rhythms.

Out in an enclaved countryside
the tempest eases,
to reveal a plough-linked atavism
steadfastly upheld.
And with it, there is kinship,
fraternity, discipline and toil
to bond a people, whose faces
bespeak a commitment to earth.

Farmsteads with interiors
severely unadorned,
stand unthreaded,
to the gifts of modernity.
Yet preside over silo,
stable and great wooden barn,
Beside gardens edged bountifully,
if incongruously, with flowers.

West Montrose on a clearing day

Elmira - a kindly flavoured town

The calm breath of life
regains its hold,
at West Montrose
on a clearing day;
black-liveried man chats amiably,
his buggied horse holds still,
afront the country store
above Ontario's last covered bridge.

And so to Elmira
- a kindly-flavoured town -
where the rain has sent
God's own stern people.
They move about together,
parted by gender, or alone,
from stable to store, to stable
to home, in utter sobriety.

The tap-roots strike
deep into rich Ontario soil,
astride the river valleys
of the Grand and Conestoga
of a people, whose people,
sojourned in rugged Pennsylvania,
and ultimately hailed from
the Rhineland's grand Palatinate.

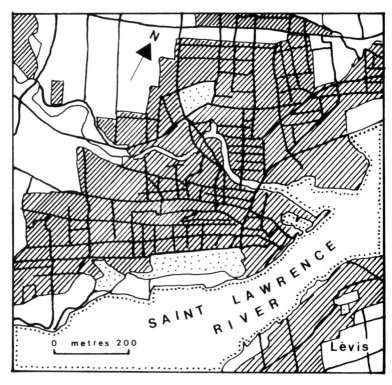

Quebec: place where the river narrows

Downtown from Upper Town

Sunday Morning Quebec

High fortress stands
above the Downtown,
challenging early morning eyes
along Rue de la Couronne.
What's in or to this Upper Town
questions the inner voice.
The reply comes reflex-like,
pick up pace and climb.

Beyond the bold promontory
steep gradients make a mockery
of two dimensional plan in hand,
amid a quiet world of saints.
Their names proclaim
streets of character,
where hardly a sinner stirs
on a morning gathering into day.

The calling bell
transmits its coded message,
unheeded by all except
the old and the afflicted,
who filter early into Mass.
Others join belatedly,
and all together yield thin ranks
from among a diminished faithful.

Street where hardly a sinner stirs

A family comes together
out of the scatter in attendance,
and lovelight in the eyes of seven
glows over a gathered people.
There's hope for onward Sundays in
a son's tribute,
a priest's blessing,
a congregation's calm acclaim.

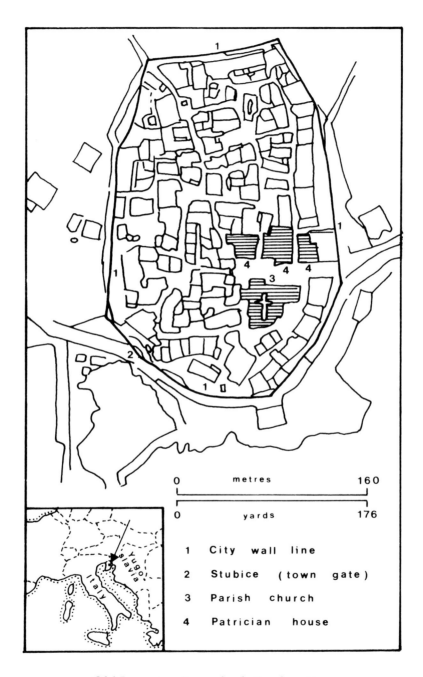

Old Lovran: site and relative location

16

Old Lovran

This is a world
within the one-time bind of walls,
with church for centre.
Come inside at Mass-time
to the stale smell of sanctity,
and the dank interior set aglow
with the waxing of lighted candles.
Old women fan their faces,
and children read and sing,
the praises of the Lord.

Frescoes on the walls
make as bold a statement
as to brush stroke
- through cycle and through legend -
Christ's and Mary's life,
from unremembered medieval imaginings;
and scenes from the Day of Judgement
come complete with the period play,
of galleries of angels,
upon strings.

Outside in the Piazza del popolo
Patrician houses signify, in cut
stone, the best of earlier days.
Their fissured fronts
make beds for darting swallows
who three-quarters black
out the sky at eventide:
and the tutelary spirit of St. George,
on a horse, moves off
from base, to all-encompass place.

The hearth of old Lovran

Away through tortuous streets
flowers run and run,
to catch the kitchen smells of Istria.
Cut back from court
where children play the tightest ball game
ever seen; to market place
where women haggle over every transactional thing;
to outer gate at Stubice,
and down steep steps,
to the sea.

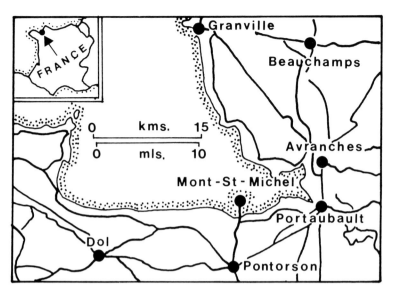

Mont St-Michel: situation and relative location

See it from a distance

Mont St-Michel

A granitic rock hewn with vision
and surrounded by quicksand,
resort of the unremembered pilgrim
dragged down by swallowing sands.
See it now only from a distance
at Avranches or Portaubault.
The close-up fails to yield the magic,
- only the hungry hordes of tourists
and the boxed merchants who peddle
baubles along the streetway to the summit.

All the magic has surely gone
at the home of the Archangel.
The Angelus bell at noon rings out
and not a sinner among the hordes
pays heed or homage.
It was never thus in Irish meadowland,
when wafting breezes brought the Angelus
to men armed with hayforks.
All life stopped in obeisance:
in another world,
a sop of hay away,
from this crowded rock in Normandy.

21

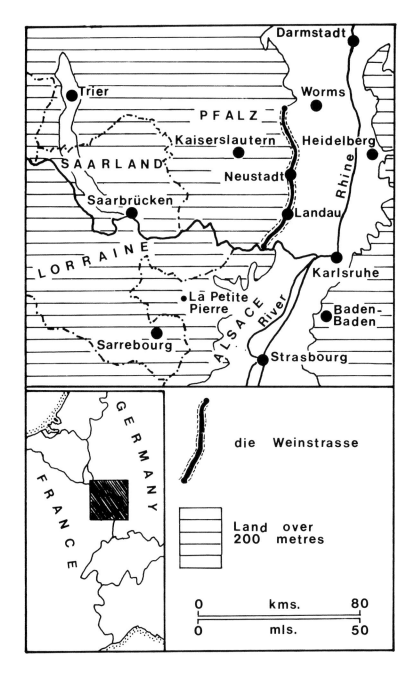

La Petite Pierre and the Franco-German borderland

La Petite Pierre

The quest for antecedent places
to fit a colonising people
is best undertaken with circumspection,
if not diversion, as I learned
when tracking the Irish Palatines.
We decided to make a break of it.
Our young son caught the sense of it.
"Daddy must be in the holiday mood,
I met him on the stairs this morning:
he wasn't talking to himself,
and he didn't give out to me."
Cross-country to Rosslare,
Cross-current to Le Harve,
we overnighted in Normandy.
Giving Paris a wide berth,
we motored towards the oscillating
borderland between Germany and France:
fixing upon a resort in the Vosges country
of Alsace, but overshooting right
up to the German line, before sideling
back on speck to La Petite Pierre.
Right on cue for the weekend
of the bi-centenary of a Revolution,
the inns were found to be as full
as the most famous of all families
had found them, except for one last chance
in the middle of a postcard
picture of a village.

Hotel Geyer

Domain to embellish a medieval chateau

24

Hotel Geyer became our base
for a fortnight of forays
into life and land in provincial France
and for overbordering into Germany:
Through *das Weintor*, along *die Weinstrasse*,
and out into the collateral field of vision:
but finding little, apart from viticulture,
to make the linkage with the husbandmen
and vinedressers who came to Ireland in 1709.
This was no land to stop and linger in,
unlike the Alsatian village where we stayed:
I wandered down the street of a morning,
driving on the wrong side of the road
to the wry amusement of all and sundry.
I would have been blasted to hell in Germany.
Then there was the sense of place
and possibility in a village
where our host, Monsieur Geyer, was mayor:
and there was ample evidence to suggest
that his family had struck deepest roots
in this, the loveliest of bosky domains
to embellish a medieval chateau.
From start to end my mind turned
to Philip Geyer, the most famous of all
the Palatines to set foot in Ireland.
"The man who drove the divil out of Ballingrane"
could only have stemmed
from a place as special as this.

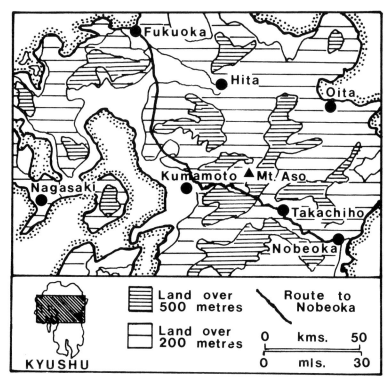

Fukuoka-Nobeoka

Nobeoka By Bus

(for Aisling)

Beyond the expressway to Kumamoto
the hills track us all the way to the Pacific,
with their constant repetition of U-bend and S-bend,
making room only grudgingly for the valley of the Gokase,
into which the road beds down,
tight against the schedule.

Asahi's striped chimney proclaims a city,
and a girl stepping out of a vision
meets us at the station.

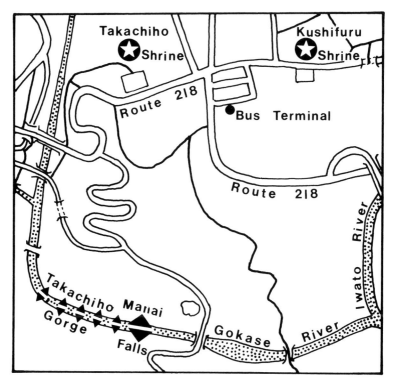

Takachiho in close-up

Takachiho

(for Shuei Ono)

The Gods came down from heaven
and made in their own likeness
the ideal country.
They filled their earthly pleasure
with the lava flows of Aso,
and they tempered the act of rapid cooling,
with the protracted play of water
upon rocks. Spending aeons
on a chasm.

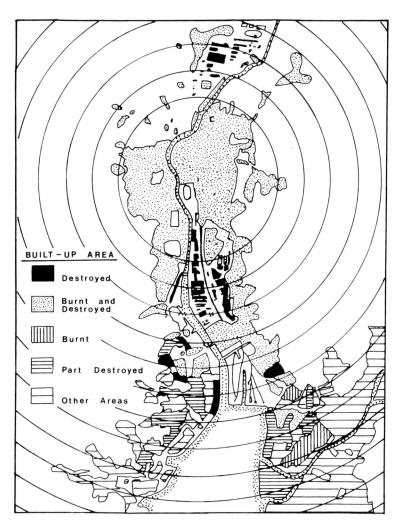

*Atomic blitz of Nagasaki, 9 August 1945, in which 73,884
people died, 74,909 were injured, and 120,820 were left
homeless*

Nagasaki Time

No artefact
in the whole wide world
records time
with the same searing precision
as the museumised clock
of Nagasaki.

It stopped
dead, in its tracks of a morning,
- August ninth,
nineteen and forty-five -
when all hell was dropped
upon earth.

Shinkansen (bullet train) against Mount Fuji

On Japan: Empire of Signs

Shinkansen against Mount Fuji:
icons of modernity and of eternal verity
proclaim a supremely coded land.
Able to absorb extraneous influences
and mutate these, if need be,
the sun also rises on this island domain:
to shed a light pure and unrefracted
on a people who have nurtured
old societal and cultural forms
in a hold-all through to post modernity.

To take the culture of the rice fields
and urbanise that culture
is no mean measure of achievement.
To take the gift of insularity.
and radicalise it on the global stage
is the wonder of our time.

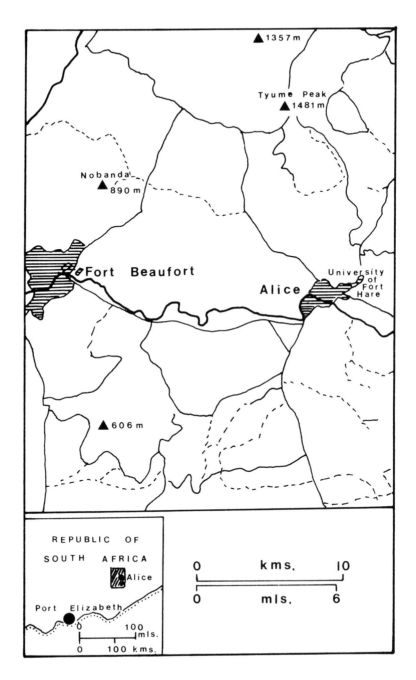

Alice: a place in the Ciskei

34

A Town Like Alice

A place in the Ciskei full of black faces
on a Friday afternoon - pay day.
Battered, degraded, reduced to shadows of itself.
The streets are full of Xhosa,
full of image and idiom.
We are just passing through
looking for *The Wrath of the Ancestors*,
available only here at Lovedale Press.
The queries and the search begin
in the countered and high-shelved setting
of the university bookshop.
For this is the home of Fort Hare,
the Oxford of Black Africa,
the intellectual cradle of Mandele, Hani and Mugabe.
A university now oddly and defensively set
in a town where life and learning diverge.

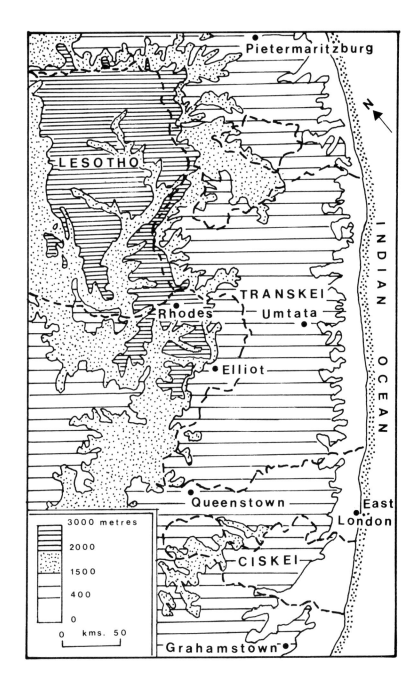

Rhodes next Lesotho in southern Africa

36

Rhodes next Lesotho

(for Colin Lewis)

The stars of an African sky
were clear as crystal.
A child could catch the stars
with a tongs and pull one down,
so luminous was the night.
Frost glistened over the ghost-like forms
of a town named after the mystery man
of a continent, here on a plateau
of the high Drakensberg.
In the transported old world ambience
that is the inn, electricity had just arrived
to light up corners never visited
before by tilley lamp or open fire.
Four poster beds were all of a period piece.
In the bar farmers of the out-country
and a policeman argued the politics
of the latest atrocity in a border corridor
where one settler had stopped one bullet
often enough to fuel the drift of desertion.
No blood should ever be shed
in so beautiful a land.

Next morning a Lesothan horseman
touched the frosts of the Rhodean town
and transcended its vision.

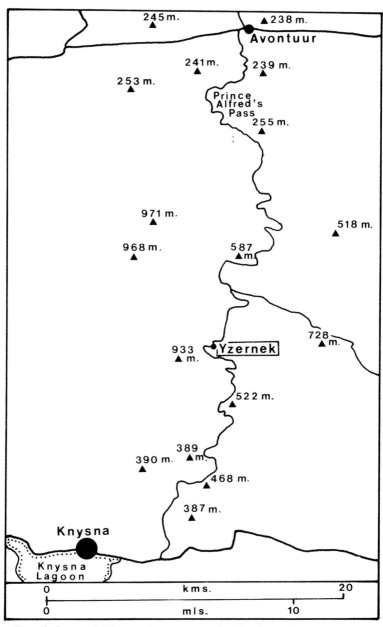

Road through Yzernek overseen by ' a little known man
from a little known townland ' circa 1859-64

Iron Pass

Nothing and no one could reveal it
till one night in the Cory Library
the pages of a book
fell open like a crib
and there at last was Yzernek.

Surveying the pass of iron in the field
beneath lay the great loop of a road
mortised in the cultured wilderness of Africa
by a little known man from a little known townland.
It was a moment of brimming.

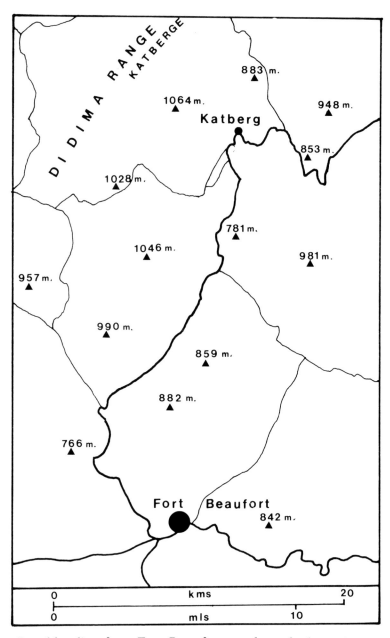

Road leading from Fort Beaufort northwards through the Katberg Pass

40

Striking North for Katberg

To span the spectrum of endeavour
as revealed by one Christopher Miller,
we struck off of a Sunday
from Grahamstown. Past old way stations,
Fort Brown and the Great Fish River,
through a narrow strip of Ciskei
and Fort Beaufort, we ascended
to the sanctuary of Hotel Katberg.
Beyond the road wove upwards
through corkscrew and switchback
evoking images to fetch the traveller
back to pioneering maker.

Then at the top of the Pass,
the line straightened for Queenstown;
the landscape took on a montane look;
and Black Africa passed by on foot.

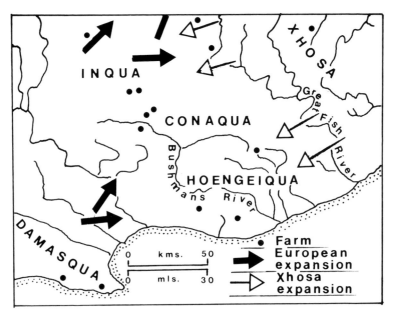

Location of peoples, late eighteenth century

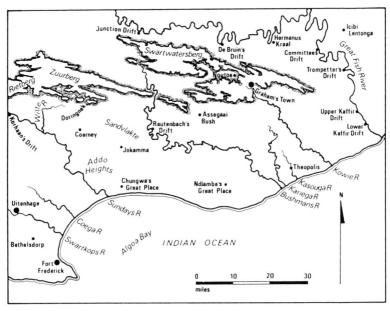

The Zuureveld 1812-1819

1820 Settler Country

I

Before it became,
it was, a borderland
with its own peoples and pain.
For the Dutch it meant
Zuureveld, the sour field,
that stretched all the way
from the Bushmans to the Great Fish River.
It lay a land, there for the taking,
by contrivance or convention,
of the predatory mind.
The English under Graham swept it up,
with as much terror as he thought fit,
for a new accommodation.
Then history took a turn.
After the Corsican had departed the European scene,
it emptied people of the Home Countries
on to distant land(s)
made by brokers peddling images.
Like pictures from fairyland,
the sour field translated
into a whole succession of English parks
to bait the homing colonist.

Markers of conquest and civility: part of Knobel's printed map of Albany, 1820

II

Entering into states of preparedness
with chain and compass,
the surveyor took the sober view
and the measure of the country.
Accounting it all in marginalia,
fine pasturage, devoid of all indigenes,
and neutral ground: since the last convention
with Xhosa chiefs made of it,
a receptacle, fit for his master's colonists.
And this (K)nobel man detailed
inside the territorial frame,
an amalgam of hachuring and fingering,
to go with rivers and their wandering
across a speckled vegetative plain.
There was nothing of a world that counted,
other than, in passing, the former seats
of Xhosa chiefs. A new heroic landscape
silenced an old, and markers of conquest
and civility turned the sour field
into the sweet, smiling land of Albany.
Then the surveyor set out a cadastral plan
to fit the face of that smiling land.

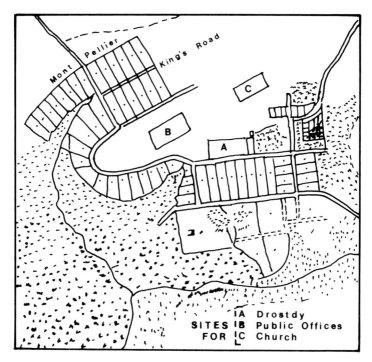

Knobel's plan of Bathurst, July 1820

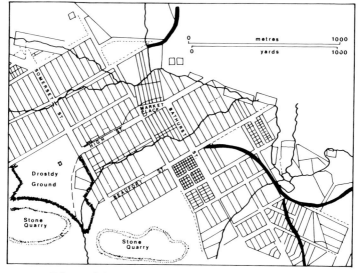

Plan of Grahamstown, circa March 1824

III

And they came, the four thousand or so,
into Algoa Bay, making their way
over slow days in ox wagons
to a land of promise,
tempered by the grind of experience.
At Assegai Bush women at odds
with the sun -and homesick- wept bitter tears,
as their men sought the shade of acacia,
to pitch tents against a single night
stand in a landscape of fear.
Then all dispersed to their locations,
tending to the land and coming
towns and villages. The colonial impress
struck home with power in the delivery.
Whether at Grahamstown, Bathurst or Cuylerville,
names on the land
betokened new and acceptable shapes,
and states of mind, transported as baggage,
to fit simplistically a tip
of the Cape of best hopes.
Thus new biographies of place
were spawned across a re-encoded plain.

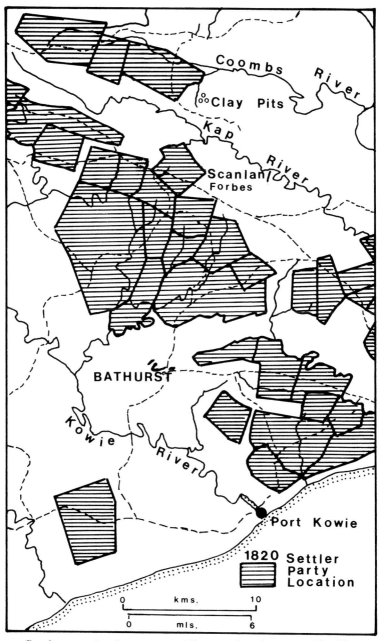

Settler parties in eastern Albany, showing specifically
William Scanlan's location and its proximity to the Clay Pits

IV

Not that anything came easy.
Far from it, as aridity gave way,
on occasion, to torrential visitation.
Land had to be made,
and re-made. And so had habitation:
from wattle-and-daub to *Devonshire cob*,
or to Boer-like walls of tempered clay.
Rust repeatedly doomed crops in the field;
desertions from the land abounded;
and overriding all, government promise
failed spectacularly to match government performance.
There were wars to contend with the Xhosa
breaking over and over an unstable frontier,
where men such as William Scanlan or Alexander Forbes
had come from out of Longford, Ireland,
to settle near the Clay Pits of Xhosa ceremonial.
Hardened by trial and by turn of occupancy,
the settlers made their own mythologies
and fashioned their own narratives:
to the exclusion of all others
recruited to stand and toil,
and settle one day in underclass location.

THE 1820 SETTLERS NATIONAL MONUMENT

The Monument was designed by J. Lamond Sturrock and was built by Murray and Roberts (E.P.) (Pty) Ltd.

VITAL STATISTICS
1970 -1974

Cost :	R5,25 million
Excavation :	15 000 cubic metres earth
	6 000 cubic metres solid rock
Concrete :	12 000 cubic metres
Steel :	432 tons
Bricks :	485 000 building bricks
	815 000 face bricks
Roofing :	6 900 square metres
Doors :	400
Auditorium Ceiling ribs (placed end to end) :	1,8 kilometres
Auditorium Ceiling joints (placed end to end) :	1,7 kilometres
Acoustic ceiling panels :	6 000 square metres
Drainage pipes :	3,3 kilometres
Water pipes (placed end to end) :	3 kilometres
Rainwater pipes (placed end to end) :	1 kilometre

Take in the conspicuous consumption

V

To move from the frontier
to the apartheid city and beyond
without crossing the street
is a neat trick of historiography
that symbolises the settlers' ideas
of themselves and of others.
Go to Grahamstown, the hearth of settler country,
and see this time-space continuum
played out along the axial line
of Cathedral to Drostdy Gate
to central arch of Rhodes University.
Proceed further to Fort Selwyn and Settlers Monument
and take in the conspicuous consumption
on sculpture, fountain, theatre and mural.
Ponder the words cited from St. John.
"That all might have life
and have it more abundantly,"
while scanning the great sweep of the polarity
of Fingo village, Makana's Kop,
and the whole conflated crescent of Rhini township.
It all passes without signing. St. John
might as well have wasted his words on the desert.

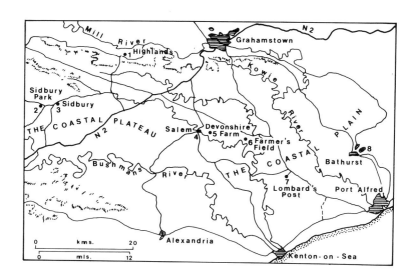

A traverse of 1820 Settler Country

Toposcope above Bathurst
52

VI

All around in Albany place-names and farm names
tell a story, remarkable for its exclusivity,
of English occupancy, harking back to 1820.
Take a traverse of a day, first to Highlands
to see a smiling valley and in the field
of peripheral vision a farm school battered
in form and facility, but full of the life
of Xhosa children and the promise of learning.
Carry on to Sidbury Park,
to the grand design of Daniell's,
and beyond it the stiff lines of a village
broken now by the choreography of black faces.
Move on to Salem and resonances
of a green village gathered on African soil
that cedes now its most venerable church
to the incantatory power of the Blacks.
Pick up in transit Devonshire Farm and Farmersfield
and the tight assemblage of Lombard's Post,
before going last to the toposcope above Bathhurst
where spoils, once allocated, are now re-presented
through three hundred and sixty degrees of the compass.
Below the township awaits the elections.

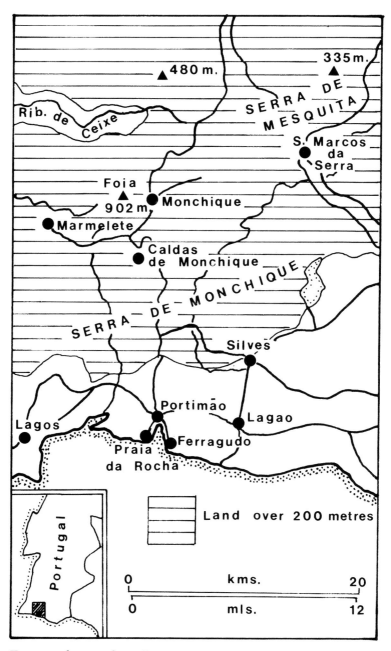

Ferragudo: out from Portimáo and everywhere in Portugal

54

Ferragudo

He stands on the corner of Hotel Jupiter
off Avenue Tomas Cabreira in Praia,
every night from nine.
A little man,
a little like Louie de Palma from *Taxi*,
except that his mission is very different.
He is the seller of his brother's paintings.
"My brother, the artist, he very tired,
he work the whole summer "
painting oils on canvass of local scenes,
some of which he brings majestically to life,
including Ferragudo.
We fix on it with a rare intensity,
and we buy it.

A hill-top village runs straight to sea
on a flank of the Rio Arade.
The conjunction of land and water,
settlement and sail,
is always intriguing,
and so are the people,
who span domains
of earth and sea.

And so we set off for Ferragudo,
for the life in the painting,
and we find it in the fishing village,
out from Portimáo,
and everywhere in Portugal,
proclaimed by its heighted church,
and skirted by its fort,
the twin of Praia.

Proclaimed by its heighted church

Skirted by its fort

56

The boats are in the harbour,
and on the harbour front
men gut and braai fish
for people such as us,
except that we are already filled
With the prospect of the massing village,
full of cobbled stairways
and sainted streets.
We ascend through eye-blink views
to find the gift of voices
from out of a little house.
It is a cobbler
and his friend,
hurtling out the vernacular
in splurges, as wild
and wonderful as the sea.

The crowning jewel
is the Virgin's church,
where the willows weep
for many a disaster.
The anchor is its emblem.
And within its precincts
are the images of a pantheon
of saints, given by the fishermen,
for their deliverance.
This we learn from a woman
in the mountains of Monchique,
who was baptised and communioned here.
This is still her little church.
Its bell rings out on the hour
and the half-hour,
and its fading coat of white
and yellow speaks now in muted tones
to the Pope in Rome.

Rua Dr. Luiz António dos Sanctos

We descend by the cobbles
of Rua Dr. Luiz António dos Sanctos
where sleeping dogs lie,
and houses are garlanded
with saints and with blossoms.
An old arthritic woman
picks tea-towels in
from the shower
that falls on children
racing home from school.

Our day clears and ends
in the Piazza,
where we sit down to a meal
of salad and sardines,
in a world as off-beat as this:
an old begging dog
sits behind us
dropping saliva in his longing,
and an oul' fella
smokes a cigarette through his nose,
saving the last pull only,
for his mouth.